Silver Linings

Reflections of Life and Hope
Through Poetry

By LaVan Robinson & Lisa Tomey

Silver Linings – Reflections of Life and Hope Through Poetry

ISBN: 978-1-7365620-1-7

Publisher: Prolific Pulse Press LLC

Library of Congress Control Number: 2021908541

Editor: Lisa Tomey

Author Photo: Larry LaVan Richardson Jr.

                Lisa Tomey

Cover Art: Lisa Tomey – Photo sourced: Unsplash

Internal Graphics: Pixabay and Private Stock

Author inquiries: prolificpulse@gmail.com

U.S.A.

TABLE OF CONTENTS

x

DEDICATION

Silver Linings is dedicated to expressions of reflections of life and hope through poetry. What we hope is that humankind will support humanity, connecting hearts, and souls for change.

To humanity, please love and stop the insanity.

To our beautiful family and friends who are like family. Love you much.

To God with whom all things are possible.

INTRODUCTION

Silver Linings came about after a discussion between LaVan AKA LaLa and Lisa. Both of us have had many concerns about society. It is important to find that ray of hope when life does not seem hopeful. Otherwise, it becomes easy to fall into depression and a sense of hopelessness can take over.

In all of life, it is important to have an outlook of positivity, even in the face of a challenging reality. Silver Linings was created to help illustrate this through poetry.

The beginning of the book has poetry by both LaVan and Lisa in collaboration. Following this are poems by LaVan and responses to each poem by Lisa.

In the last portion of the book there are individual poems by LaVan and Lisa.

Turning it Around to Hope

Seeking silver linings of any gray cloud seemed
impossible

with the world at each other's throats with no peace in
sight.

It made me wonder if there was a way that is possible

to lift this world from the deep well of continuous strife.

I pulled back from the news, turned off the TV

opened my horizontal blinds, raised them up high

Sunbeams entered my home, dust flying free

when I realized that it was up to me to turn off the blight.

I dug deep within me to draw off the power—

immediately my whole perspective

changed within the amazing hour.

The morning had dawned my new beginning

to the renewal of life which was reborn.

Awakening Humanity

With no regard to the goodness of life
one more day, we lose another.
The guns blast, the tempers flare.
Where does the end come to this strife?

Politicians battle over linguistics
while the street battles are personal.
Another life is taken, none given
with no regard to the goodness of life.

Another one was taken while trying to breathe
discourse--puts it mildly while anger,
fills every part of this existence.
How can we find a way for this to leave?

Flip the switch to the bright lights

burning in our eyes, reflecting discord.

Understand what people fear when

another one was taken while trying to breathe.

Let's be better than this, brothers, and sisters,

let's find the way past this, somehow.

Answers start when we can listen to each other

with total regard that pain is being inflicted.

Humanity is in a battle to be won

without regard to the full worth of persons.

We cannot go back and let history repeat.

Let's be better than this, brothers, and sisters.

Moving forward to a better way

that'll promote in humanity—

a spiritual awakening,

that'll lead to extending love and

self-respect in our lives and days.

Actions

We, humanity meet at the destined gathering place where we discuss, reflect, and solve issues that we face as one human race. Our actions have hindered the positive advancement and caused so much pain. Despite this terrible fact, there's much still to be gained. We're in this wholeheartedly together and it's up to each one individually to do their part to contribute to the betterment of this world and of the soul true purpose. The key to life itself lies deep within our physical surface. Challenges are meant to test where your loyalty lies and to make or break that which is inside. You're beautiful in the most divine way and are given a chance to add to or leave a legacy every day. Use your time here to acquire wisdom, knowledge, understanding, love, and compassion. Become a light in the darkness in the struggle, survival, and blessings in the everlasting journals of humanity written and recorded actions.

LaLa

Gather for the Light

We gather as one human race

ready to face the challenges.

Hey, it's in the face.

No ready, just getting right with

humankind.

Each one, teach one, so they say.

Whole hearts,

whole souls,

beautiful souls,

gaining wisdom,

gaining knowledge,

gaining understanding,

love, and compassion.

Make that light shine.

This little light of mine...

all day long.

Unwoke folks better be willing

to learn.

They aren't the teachers here.

Lisa

Ad Lib

We're all actors in the production called life. The world is our stage where our purpose is scripted out and played. Seldom do we get to have input in the fabric of its makeup. If things don't go according to our way, we have a chance to change the overall outcome of life itself, every day. The director of life has given each actor their own personal script and a roadmap to traverse their path to their existence and validity. You can dictate what roles you decide to take on raising the bar to that of superstar. Life will test you to see just how serious and strong you really are. Remember while you're here, use wisely your special talent and gift because you and only-you when it comes to your soul and life-can ab lib.

LaLa

Hope Takes Me Far

Hope comes to mind

when life gets tough

when I realize it's mine

to mess up.

When I make mistakes

and you know that I will

I need to step up the faith

and let hope ascend the hill.

I write my own script.

I make my own plans

and if I need a lift

I know you understand.

Talents are abundant

just finding the right niche

to emerge triumphant

is to find the ultimate.

But when I flounder

and need to have a lift

hope places me further

and I will get a grip. ~ Lisa

Advancement

I ignite words using a very eccentric inner soul beat. The way they're formatted and arranged will have the average person giving three finger snaps praising God dancing and shouting in the streets. I try to do it just a little better than those who graced this beautiful earth before me. Uniquely bringing about self-awareness, wisdom, knowledge, and understanding through the timeless gift of poetry. Becoming the voice to those deemed voiceless desperately needing and wanting to expose all who practice the art of manufacturing and imposing upon the meek and weak their evil choices. Gladly giving reference, recognition, and honor to the Heavenly Father whose gifts he distinctively gave to me. Using it for the spiritual, mental, and physical advancement of positiveness for all humanity.

LaLa

Souls Matter

No holding back was the plan, when turning words into phrases, each meant to make a difference in humanity. Facing the challenge of saying the right things, served to be more difficult in these ages. When younger, I was always sensitive to the feelings of people, cringing at expressions I heard, sometimes in my own environment. Now, I continue to choose my words carefully. But what of it if there is a meaning I may have misunderstood and some poor soul finds my words to be hurtful, then I must do what I can to remedy this. But, oh I desire to honor the souls of people and to shed light on what is damaging to other souls. It is my hope that I choose these words carefully for advancement of goodness in this world. It is complicated, but it is necessary, for the hope of souls of all who will allow change and who will allow chance and who will allow enrichment. And this is the community I desire the most.

Lisa

Anew

Under the fluorescent light, I sit quietly at a table and wonder. Reminiscing about all the trials and tribulations I had to go through what was meant to take me six feet under. Yes, I was so low it seemed that the ants could—with one hop—jump over me. There was for me no hope as I plunged deeper and deeper into the grips of dope. I was willing to throw everything that mattered like caution into the blustery wind. Every time I thought I had beaten my demons, it had become more prevalent, bigger and badder—time and time again. Just when I was at my very lowest and all seemed lost, God then showed himself and proclaimed that for my soul, he had paid the ultimate cost. Took my hand leading me to his fold and from that moment on, I was engulfed by his love, mercy and grace that healed my once embattled and embittered soul. Now a new song I have in my heart, and of a loving God I am now a part, and my road is set from which I again will never depart. So, when times are hard and you're at the ropes end, you can call on God and immediately your life change will begin.

LaLa

Trust

Trusting in another soul takes everything I have.

Years of disappointment made me hesitant to believe.

It took a long, hard look at the person who I became.

To be ready to make changes and to accept the best of me.

Years later, I am still growing from life's experiences.

I learned to trust better and look over new fences.

Faith in what I was meant to be, helped me to know.

I had to let go of some of the old to grow, anew.

Lisa

Answering My Prayers

Through the fog of life's despair, it is your sweet angelic voice that I gravitate to and hear. You are my shining star providing much needed light and laying my eyes upon your beauty is my soul's perfect delight. Oh, so many aren't given this a once in a lifetime chance to experience or to be blessed with a romance such as ours--my strong and vibrant love--who I haven't met yet but I'm always dreaming of. The very thought of you always makes me so privileged and more and more giving me hope and a true reason to live. I thank God for hearing and answering my prayers and bestowing upon me finally the woman that has so long occupied my dreams and made her to be an integral part of my life and reality.

LaLa

Prayers Well Heard

As I sat in my home, warm and happy, it was, I still knew there was something missing. That something was one true love. While my life was fine as it stood, I knew having a special someone to share with would make it better. And along came you, not expectedly. As the expectations I had were surpassed. With a purely clear soul, one I wanted to warm to, I felt like my hopes, my heart, my prayers were heard. And it is true. The one person I wanted in my life is the person known as you. Now we have been together for a few years and hope for many more, but as we age, we know it's not the same as before. It's better, closer, richer than we could ever hope for and now we have our evermore.

Lisa

Appointed Day

Moving forward to days that are slowly becoming more and more bleak.

Investing in the business of hate and hoping that this way of living never ceases.

For humanity it's sealed its fate by its own means and that isn't up for debate.

Do people care that causing pain on one another is the only thing they have in common and-as a whole-really share?

Comfortable in this stagnant state of despair, chasing vanity as the earth is responding negatively from years and years of wear and tear.

Remember, this is our home and as one humanity, we must take care of it before its appointed day with being thrown into hell's fiery pit.

LaLa

Turn it Around

I want to turn around the way this day has started out.

The power is in my hands to enable change.

Turning humanity around means looking at myself.

Pain in my neighbor's life means pain in my own.

Let's not get comfortable with stagnation and let's choose change.

Together— humanity can be joined together for the same cause.

Lisa

Appreciation

Love can conquer all, so when faced with adversity, you must be ready to heed to its call. Uplifting the wretched soul from the pitfalls of life can set it anew and on high. Giving children of men a positive reason to be. And for another with hope and resilience a beacon. Providing perfect counsel through the darkness that on one's life tragically fell upon. Navigating, encouraging, and strengthening your spiritual, mental, and physical ties and bond, closer you will be to God; when you find your peace that dwells inside and have a greater appreciation for love in your life.

LaLa

Seeking Answers

Faced with decisions

between the road of despair

and the road most calm

which one will we choose today?

Seeking soulful counseling

answers come with prayer

as we seek spiritual counsel

for decisions here.

In the nowness of this life

what gray areas are there?

Seek hope to survive.

Seek resilience to endure.

Seek life to give heart.

Seek eternal peace inside

and live life to the fullest.

Lisa

Be

I give honor to those brave and beautiful souls that paved the way for me to follow and positively promote the beauty of my blackness. The blueprint is simple, we as one people must unite and for our existence, we must stand and fight for equality. All must be included in the plan to uplift humanity. Every soul in the continuation of struggle truly matters and that's a fact. When it's all said and done, accountability for actions or lack of, will be in the forefront. Treat one another in love, respect and with dignity and only then will this nation and others around the world and all its inhabitants experience, realize and taste the beneficial qualities of what others did and continue boldly laying down their lives for to see into fruition one man's vision of the simplicity of the powerful dream of how we could truly live and be.

LaLa

Those Before Us

With honor I regard the peacekeepers

in a world with so much pain.

There have been leaders of great stature

who have led the way from shame.

When regarding those who keep the peace

keep in mind those who keep quiet.

Living their lives in ways of love

and keeping their bases solid for respite.

Not all people march and hold court

but they hold something else.

Everything they see and hear

becomes an influence on decisions.

And if those decisions mean peace

and motivate them to keep watch—

then those before us are just as much

as those who exist in every day.

Bringing peace in our daily lives

pay attention to the helpers

of this world—

They hold the keys to peace. ~ Lisa

Beast

The plot thickens as end time nears. During which the boyz will be playing off its citizens many fears. Perpetrating lies just to continue to control lives. Watch what they do—not what they say—and you'll see that in your life they want plenty of clouds of darkness and grey. Many to them will fall victim. All planned by the beast who's behind and secretly controlling their system. This has been in the works for some time where first they will control your soul and then your mind. To the beast many will give their total allegiance and ultimate power too. Joining its campaign to destroy the fabric of humanity and send it to its doom. In this era, hold on to your faith and God will lead the way, diverting the path to destruction and providing a much better and brighter day.

LaLa

Beast and Brethren

What is happening with the end of time wars?

It's not the table where my meals are eaten

But brother, it's happening for sure at yours

What is the reason we are crossing these paths?

We must always be mindful of each person's pains—

remembering the past and how much we've gained

and when the opportunity comes—make change.

Rights, to be civil have been fought in the past

and we can't just say that these concerns left.

No sir, no ma'am, there is much more to do here.

Let's keep our larders stocked and welcome our kin—

brothers and sisters with all colors of skin.

Keep your faith and be mindful that life is ours

only when we are willing to give of our hours.

Hold on to hope and give faith and works a chance.

Lisa

Bliss

If you see things with your heart, then deep within you a spiritual change will start. The beauty in all things you will find and to the blessings around, you won't be blind. In you, the seeds of love will grow and happiness you will begin to sow. Spreading its joy all throughout the land even extending it to the enlightenment of man. For this is the true path to success and living your life in total peace and bliss.

LaLa

Peace

seeking peace within

soothing the soul with prayer

contemplating life

engaging the heart in joy

spiritual change begins

sowing seeds of peace

watering them thoroughly

tending to the weeds

one by one they grow up high

bearing fruits of goodness

such is life, you see

tilling the soil and planting

seeds which have purpose

and they become seeds of peace

when given nurturing love

Lisa

Countless Lives

America and its bewildered citizens are at a spiritual crossroads. So many have already given up their precious souls. Believing and taking the leaders for their words, but actions speak for themselves or haven't you heard? Every day it seems to be getting worse as many are willing to spill innocent blood just to quench their insatiable thirst. Their agenda for the New America is plain and clear. Divide and conquer instilling fear and more fear. Nothing seems like this pattern is going to end as it settles in as the new fad and trend. We must continue-no matter how hard it gets-to fight as long there is breath in our souls to save countless lives.

LaLa

Fight

They say nobody

should spend all their life in pain

because they are hated.

Yet the hatred of mankind

spends lives as if they're worthless.

Why should a life be

spoiled like rotted meat in the sun

to gain the power

of a weak society

just to prove a point.

No, stand and stand tall

fighting with our might for peace.

Souls are worth more than

rotted meat in high noon sun.

They are worth the fight to love.

Lisa

Cultivation

The conscious mind is the fertile soil in which the seeds and thoughts of the unconscious grows into fruition and are made into reality. If you don't cultivate the soil, then it will be overwhelmed by the weeds of doubt and stagnation. The time and energy you put into the care of your soul and being will sprout very amazing, powerful, beautiful, breathtaking, and spellbinding flowers of sensory delights and enlightenment beautifying all around its benevolent presence.

LaLa

Truth

Bearing fruit requires a strong foundation, roots deep in the soil, nourished with the fuel of life, saturating, encouraging growth. So much goes on that we cannot see, but rest assured, the workings are happening. Analogous with the minds of youth, what you see with your eyes are not always their truths. Roots run deep. Honesty, trust bind into those roots of growth. Let the ties that bind be strong, nourished with the fuel of life, not just water, but the deep, deep wisdom of knowing the essence of pure bloodlines of growth. This is how the roots become wings and how our youth can have hope.

Lisa

Disappear

Beauty is more than what the eyes can see. Its roots are based on what in someone—is within deep. There's beauty in everything. There's beauty in the way birds chirp and sing. There's beauty in how the ants go about gathering and preparing for the winter during the summer or early spring. There's beauty in the trees of how large they grow and filter the air that's helps us to breathe. There's beauty in the mystical sea from all the magnificent creatures and species it provides so abundantly. There's beauty everywhere you go and when nourished properly, it can help the earth and its wonderful landscapes to become vibrant and grow. You don't have to go far to see the positive and everlasting effects of its great blessings. I hope we as humanity take the time out to truly see and smell the beauty of the roses—we oh so love to give and share—before it and all, from our actions, that are so negative, disappear.

LaLa

The Earth is Warming

Two or more ways to destruction of all

Globally, the heat is blazing so strong

responding to manmade fires from rageful

people who are misled and misleading.

Now, the fire burns innocent wildlife

only because of ignorance turned loose.

Innocent animals are running scared.

Houses are burning to cremation.

It's not just set fires but the earth's response

from mankind using needless chemicals

and conserving is not in the forefront.

Recycling is slow and gardens are bare.

Using the earth for nourishment is rare.

Stopping these hard ways may help humankind.

Let's hope for change; it begins with our minds.

Lisa

Fellow Man

There are so many people in the world having a hard time dealing with life and the cards that they've been dealt. Struggling with the pain and the effects of such still so very much deeply felt. Coping and getting by the best that they can and believing that there's no one out there that understands. Feeling lost in this great big ole world, screaming for help but not being noticed or even heard. Walking around totally unresponsive to all around them. Without feeling just totally numb. Hoping for someone or anyone that'll care and their struggles and problems they can openly share. We all have things that we struggle with. It's important that we're able to rely on each other and not quit. This please do understand that we have to look out not only for ourselves but also for our fellow man.

LaLa

Is It Me?

Is it me or do you think it so

looking at the world in my little nucleus

watching how each ebb and flow

comes together

washing to shore the needs

of our fellow people

There's the lady in the store

the one about to give birth

sitting on a stool

as she runs the register

people asking for things

regardless of her condition

what to do to be kind?

What about the one

who waits while groceries are rung

tapping her foot from anxiety

noting the total

trying her card— declined

what to do to be kind?

What about the neighbor

having kids full of energy

arms full to the car

rushing and dropping

laughing and running

nerves clearly fraying

what to do to be kind?

It takes a village, so they say

as the oceans of life bring needs ashore

asking ourselves the question again

what to do to be kind?

Lisa

Final Hour

We are all shining stars suspended in the picturesque scheme of the universe. Our ambiance upon this earth, we diversely disperse through our destined gifts. Wooing and amazing others we give the downtrodden spirit an incredible jolt and uplift. We leave our perched place of high to successfully provide a blueprint to navigate safely this bittersweet road called life. Preparing our metal to be stronger, it is truly an adventure filled with both sweet and sour. Allowing us to obtain wisdom, knowledge, and understanding and to be accountable to God standing before him, in that final hour.

LaLa

The Outstretched Hand

high places are sought

in the temple of life

many want to be atop

one wonders what can be done

for others in need

who cannot climb those stairs

to the top of the temple

there are those in need

of the outstretched hand

whether they want to climb

those temple stairs

or simply want

to live life on solid ground

help them make their life livable

as told by some wise man

seek not to go

to the high places of the temple

reach out your hand to help others

be their light in life

with eyes opened to the possible

ways to help others

this is giving hope

an outstretched hand reaches out

for hope, for every soul

Lisa

Flowers Still Bloom

Despite the upheavals in a damaged society where people have yet to put its survival as a top priority, destruction, misery, and pain parading boldly in its streetz, taking out whoever is in its path causing mothers daily—to constantly weep. Leaders outright abusing the trust and power given to them by the people who expect them to do the right thing. When approached with the evidence, claiming to know not a thing, and turning on one another's life—canaries, they boldly sing. Waking up to another day where on the agenda is more gloom. I'm grateful that despite all these things and more, the flowers still bloom.

LaLa

Planting for Hope

What harvest is there
when seeds are planted in mud?
Will it drain enough
for a bountiful harvest
or drown the seeds in sorrow?

Tilling the rough, stony soil,
sifting out big rocks,
leaving some pebbles for good,
I'll save the stones for
beautiful wells of strong hope,
so as not to waste
any goodness of this earth.
Lisa

God's Sight

Unsettling times brings about unsettling thoughts. Now living in America, I must be mindful of the way I talk, act, and walk. Judging me by my color of skin I'm in and against me and mine, purposely perpetrating and manufacturing atrocities. For America, it's just business as usual and lives don't matter, only the dollar residual. With collateral damage in its wake. You can now start to see the once strong country beginning to break. With ice in its veins, the foundation and ideologies won't allow it to change freely and willingly. All people are equal and precious in God's sight so accept this or hell for this America will be its plight.

LaLa

Hope in Sight

there is hope in sight

with plans for damage control

keeping a close watch

on collateral damage

we must honor those we've lost

moments of silence

needed to maintain our stance

brothers and sisters

we are the united states

let us take a solid stand

as united souls

we are joined in a union

safety in numbers

and to remember that we

always have hope in our sight

Lisa

Healing Begin

Sadly, amongst one another there is so much hate. And the more we kill each other more problems it just seems to create. The obstacles just get bigger and bigger—every time someone settles problems by pulling the trigger. What else could it be that as brothers and sisters, we refuse to love and treat kindly? Yeah, this trajectory we have to confront and come to a better conclusion amidst all that's happening among the world's ball of misery and confusion. Learn of self, history, loving the skin you're in and only then will the true healing begin.

LaLa

Life's Stairway to Heaven

The pellets of society rush hard
and shielding becomes a necessity.
We must ask ourselves how to make the change.
Survival by might of muscle must stop.
Avoiding bullets is no way of life.

When faced with problems of this lost soul world
making an impact in my own small space
could help people claim hope in times so tough.
We all know a way we can help others.
Use that thoughtful way to strengthen their souls.

Reign high and low for humankind to live.
Let solace for each person be given.
Enforce an armor like a gold staircase.
Leading lives to find a heavenly place
on this earth and not to wait for reward.
Lisa

Heartfelt

The toolbox you possess inside of you has everything you need to navigate and see your life through. Don't give up when it seems the road is hard and full of devices to knock you off your chosen path. Keep looking to the stars above to lead the way, relying on the coordinates of the soul and with love, patience, persistence, understanding, and perseverance, you will soon make it out of the storms, turbulence, and adversity to experience brighter times and days. You will eventually reach your destination with much humbleness, gratitude, and appreciation. Becoming more knowledgeable about self and be willing unconditionally to share this wealth with those who, too, need direction with dignity and friendship that's strongly and richly heartfelt.

LaLa

Tools for Life

Tools in your life's toolbox

A hammer to pound away for determination

A wrench to tighten up resolve

A screwdriver to keep going but recognize when goals are reached

A planer to trim away the rough edges and allow for smooth transitions

A lathe to twist the barriers into beautiful hoists

A grease gun to slide off criticisms

A handbook about how to use these tools

A great band playing to support the dance of life

Lisa

Illuminating Self

All living objects are made from energy of the celestial and universal body and its alignment accordingly to the conscious of its spiritual nature. We're able to transfer that energy from within, into motion. We're also able to transmit that into whatever we feel comfortable and reside in. It then takes shape and form of the structure. Therefore, it conforms and adjusts and validates its existence. We're a mass or molecule of living energy transmitted through the soul and its mystic light. It all works in coordination with the synchronization of life. Therefore, you illuminate your self-reflection through energy.

LaLa

Keep Hope Alive

bursting wide open

the soul asked for air

breathe into me

was the internal cry

nurture me

energize me

keep me alive

it is just a matter of time

before the internal

and the external

forces collide

all I am asking

is keep hope alive

Lisa

In Thee

From the heavens above, it came pouring down upon my essence. For I was spiritually, mentally, and physically drained and so tired, so very tired and felt like I was about to expire. Just when it seemed I couldn't go much further and crawling on my knees was I. Unclear who and what it was, I felt an entity by my side. Its presence brought about in me a surge of energy and strength I never experienced. It picked me up from my knees and from there started my spiritual repentance. My essence was fully replenished and given a boundless source of hope. As my eyes cleared, I finally could see that it was the spirit of God that had come suddenly upon me. I quickly dropped back down to my knees to give it its due honor, praise, and blessings. Pleased was he that said to me now, my child, share this story among humanity because I'm now in thee.

LaLa

Reason to Hope

cherishing the nurture of the divine

allowing that which is a mystery

to combine with the breath of my life

massaging my heart and assuring me

this is the meaning of my existence

and I look to the magnificent universe

and realize that, this, all this

is yet another manifestation

of universal love

and in the deepest part of my soul

I find there truly is reason to hope

Lisa

Inner Peace

Of your reality, you're the creator. You have the power to make it much better and greater. Touching and inspiring lives and souls along the way. Providing hope into days that are hopeless and gray, whatever reality you choose all depends on what here on this earth you do. Be the light you're meant to be. Through the darkness and troubling times, you can shine so bright and illuminating. Bringing about through your destined journey to others and yourself that much needed inner peace.

LaLa

The Hope for Peace

After tilling the soil of this great land, I found a legacy. It was an old, metal, toy car. I took it to my friend, and he sandblasted it. It was soon working like new. I kept the car for many years and cherished it. In time, it passed hands to a grateful soul. It brought me great joy to pass this on. There was something aged, tossed or lost in the ground, tilled over for many years, along with many layers of memories. And when it was found, it was brought to new life. This is how I feel about the concept of peace. It takes years, generations, to establish peace in our land. It may not be seen in current generations, but in the future, it can happen. Just because we cannot touch it, or polish it up, or even sandblast it, doesn't mean it's not possible. It will have layers of memories. It will be discussed for ages. It will be worth the wait. It is an ongoing process and when the time is right, it will come forth.

Lisa

Insight

To the greatness that you seek the road has been set within the nature of your existence. You must work hard and be focused and persistent if you want to succeed to fulfill your fantasies, dreams, aspirations, and destiny. Enjoy the sunrise that God has bestowed upon humanity. Extend love to one another and believe in its power. Take time to explore the basic world around you and smell the beautiful flowers. At the sunset of your precious life, you will be elated and proud because all around you would have benefited from your greatness and insight.

LaLa

Keep Hope Alive

inroads to the deepest part of the lungs and the heart

lead to the soul, holding court, but not seen

dancing on the chest, or heaving with the breast

it sits quietly, yet desire stirs in the constant

desire for nurture and essential growth

while the soul does not live on our skin

it needs the essential elements to foster growth

walking in the light of day

breathing in the freshness of dawn

finding ecstasy in the throes of love

yes, my friend, the soul lives our lives

and it is up to us to make sure

it gets the fairest run

and embracing the fullness of life

is one way it begins

to keep hope alive

Lisa

Inspiration

In spectacular fashion is humanity made. Stemming from one entity we are all practically the same. What affects one race eventually comes back around to affect all. When one race stumbles and fall, it's up to the others to help pick each other back up to stand tall. We are in this together, so we must put aside negativity to make this world of ours so much better. Learn from the mistakes of the past and demand change so that love can make a positive impact to last. Set the standards for the next generations so they too for one another can be a game changing and everlasting inspiration.

LaLa

Generations Strong

hope keeps us going

when we see our peoplehood

for what they are now

recognizing that we all

have a place in the mansion

when we lift each other up

falling has no place

in a life where souls are held

as cherished forever

for if tomorrow

were to vanish from this life

we will feel assured in knowing

souls were honored and

generations will carry on

with the strength of cherished souls

Lisa

Much Greater and Better

The politicians are elected to power on the strength of making promises and fancy speeches. While there they abuse it, leaving behind carnage and others are left to rebuild and pick up the broken and damaged pieces. This seems to be the pattern that's set with each successor not able to make it better yet. We only have one another for this to blame by the way we treat each other. Yes, it's a darn shame. Love is the only way we can dig ourselves out of this dismal reality of a hole. There is so much at stake like the fate of humanities soul. For this cause, accepting and putting aside our differences and coming together is the only fool proof solution to make America and the rest of the world for all much greater and better.

LaLa

To Find the Way to Love in This World

My friend, it is about accepting

  Love one another by the guidance of good

putting aside our differences

  Turn your back on the ways of darkness

coming together

  Unifying for greatness

as the only fool proof solution

  Seek ways to find peace

for America and the rest of the world

  Leaving no souls untended

to be much greater and better.

  And this, my friend is how we get there

Love in this world is about making each day

A better day in which to co-exist

And really, isn't that love and peace?

Lisa

Obligation

We truly are blessed to be able to live on a beautiful planet adorned with such mystical pleasures and greatness. Its vast resources are aligned to help us all to grow physically, mentally, and spiritually. It's nutritional value also helps our everlasting light of our precious soul to brightly shine and glow. We must learn to respect this wonderful place called earth. Protect and take care of it so the other generations after can enjoy its gifts too for all its worth. We are made as its custodian. We must do a better job in the revitalization of its existence. Learn to love this amazing home that we call earth. This is our home and to keep it beautiful, we each have an obligation to see it through. To keep the sun shining and the blue skies blue.

LaLa

Evidence

Let's leave behind the evidence of hope. When years from now others we will never know, breathe the air, they will know it was because we made it possible. We are the managers of this earth, so freely given to us. Prepare what legacy we leave, the imprint we make on this our earthly gift. Tend the soil with care, being frugal with the treatments. Conserve water with concern about the next generation. Secure a place for our future genes and let them relish a land of possibilities and joy. Teach our future generations about caring for their future generations. Climate change may occur, but we are the stewards of this land and for this job we must gather and till the soil of the future.

Lisa

Setbacks

We are made with a master plan on our destiny and how we fit into the scheme of everyday existence. To be in tune to your divine purpose, you must look deep inside the operating system of the soul. When you fall off track of that purpose, God has a way of getting your attention and setting you straight once again. We call them setbacks but, it's a wakeup call. No matter how much we as humanity and individuals plan the steps, we deem necessary and vital to our happiness, we must be open to be able to adjust when our plans falter. Find your true destiny from within the standard operating procedures and from the lessons, gain the knowledge that's available that you lacked. Look for the silver lining from what we consider to be in life, setbacks.

LaLa

Reset

We are all equipped with a reset button
so, to speak. To be literally on point—
decisions once made, may need adjusted.
Second chances are meant to be heeded.
How many times I have started over
cannot be counted on one hand.
Rest assured, these changes meant lessons
learned about how and what and why and more.
Looking at the silver lining, hope comes to reality
and each day offers another chance to grow.
Lisa

Souls Beats

The rhythm of life is dictated by the beats of your soul. Within it is a precious treasure to receive and behold. You have the power to make your life lyrically sound. Adding to the orchestra of the essence that cannot be bound. Freely it's meant to flow, and others enlighten. Exposing the soul to the musical compositions that are meant to heighten.

LaLa

Caring for Souls

Expect to have nurturing in the recipe for caring for your souls. Add a depth of understanding for when lost you may sometimes feel. Give yourself compassion before you freely share. Essence of self-giving, will serve to give others their share. Always, always, hear me friend, take care of your soul. Taking what you need before letting another know. If there is a log in the eye, you cannot see your fellow ones. So, take care of your soul first. Then you will be able to offer others hope.

Lisa

The Neighborhood That We Once Knew

Illegal business trafficking boldly on the streets in broad daylight so everyone can see. The addicts are searching high, low, and even on their elbows wondering how they're going to get their next hit of crack or blow— While the hustlers are trying to get rid of the hot merchandise that they have stolen. All can't help but to see the once beautiful and vibrant neighborhood now infested with all types of rodents. Why did we the people let it get this way? It's so dangerous that it's unsafe even for children to play. It used to be a community with businesses and flowers in full bloom. Now you look around, you see abandoned homes/buildings in an area that's invaded by gloom. It seems that with the passing of time so have the people's self-esteem and pride. To make it better though, there's so much now that we all must do because we can all agree that it's a far cry from the neighborhood that we once knew.

LaLa

Finding Home

law breaking business pre-dates these modern times

for more years than I have breathed there has been crime

my own people back in the days and even the hills

found gain in the ventures with moonshine making stills

it doesn't take urban life to corner the market for loss

the soul finds its darkness in every corner crossed

uncles and cousins made their own kind of brew

and sat around and yarned about this and that too

mice ran the kitchen at night while they slept

snakes found their way in the sleeping child's bed

bare feet in creek beds found leeches on toes

sometimes it was all one could do to keep clothes

moonshine or crack, marijuana, or blow,

the centuries past have all had their woes

it's a hustle, it's a hassle, it's a survivalist game

no matter the venue, it's gonna be the same

just when you think, I have given up hope

in how the world's coming and going with dope

keep this in mind, and I assure I will too

each day I rise, I will rise for you

keep each day as sacred as I know how

never fear taking a hold on the plow

bravely stepping forward when adversity taunts

it's never in vain, time to clean up the haunts

be faithful, diligent, truthful, be strong

the temple was not built on a sweet Sunday song

Lisa

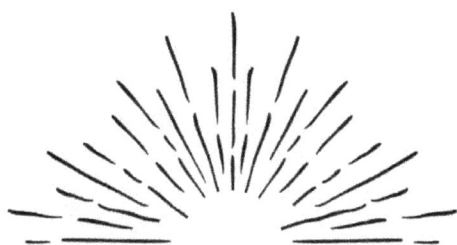

True meaning of Life

Waking up hearing the birds outside my window jubilantly sing. They dare not worry about what the day will bring. They humbly go about their business knowing that God will provide their needs as we should know that our souls with his blessings he'll feed. Tomorrow isn't promised to no one, but if you're blessed to see another day do appreciate the warmth from the rays of the sun. All your needs, trust God to provide for that's the true meaning of life.

LaLa

It's Just that Simple

open the windows

birds are communicating

music to our ears

we absorb dailies of life

nurturing souls to survive

Lisa

True Value and Worth

Giving freely that which is of the heart produces the blueprint for living righteously. You're built to endure, last, and succeed. You have the power within to dictate and navigate the treacherous journey of life. Given the wisdom, knowledge and understanding of God to know wrong from right. You're much greater than anything here on this earth. So be ever grateful and boldly rejoice knowing your true value and worth.

LaLa

Worth

when you feel the pressures of life
you must do this, that, or the other
according to the gospel of humankind
do they understand this
that we are all valuable persons
regardless of our abilities
ableism has a fault line
it is the line which implies
we are all to be the same

life's journey can be treacherous
and when the powers that be
imply that someone is lesser than
the treacherousness increases
seventy times seven
a code of ethics goes a long way
once implemented in life

then, and only then, will we realize

we are all able

I trust people will sign up for the class

Father Figge would have been proud

Lisa

Woman

I am proud of the beautiful women who have graced my life with their beauty and presence. Each moment was a learning experience and a blessing. Each one ingrained in me the power of their instruction and awareness of self. Their love was the backbone of my validation of my manhood. The principles of family and its values propelled me to become the best variation of me that God intended me to be. Through their prayers and selfless sacrifice, I continue their dream. Living as a positive example of perseverance, strength against all odds that they faced. I am grateful to all they provided me and continue to in honor of their friendship and support that cannot ever be replaced. Thank you to all the woman for you're the thread that holds it all together and makes a house into a lovin', carin', and positive structure of a home. Without your tenacity, grace, and dignity a nation wouldn't be built. For you're the mother of all humanity. You're the one and only woman.

LaLa

Daddy and Mom

teaching about how to live

a life with dignity, no shame

giving us hope for a new day

daddy, you did this with good intent

mom, you gave us backbones strong

as you showed us by your love

the paths to follow and which to avoid

our lives forever blessed by your ways

together, you two gave us a foundation

to try to make it in this, our nation

may we hope forever to bring you joy

with love, your little girls, and boys

Lisa

LaVan Robinson

A Difference

My existence was written in destiny before time. Out of a majestic and divine royalty, my being and essence was formed in kind. Love is the pleasure to indulge my passion for life. The powerful, almighty, and awesome greatness that inspires me also illuminates my soul's light. I am delighted to do his holy will. For when the arrows and bullets surround me, it is his love, grace, and peace in me that's profoundly instilled. For the advancement of humanity, I'll proudly use my gifts to become and promote the voice for the voiceless. Every life and soul matters, this I fully understand. Thank you, God, and to make a positive difference in this world for all, I am grateful for the chance.

Memories

All moments are meant to become memories. So, make sure sharing life with that special someone, family or friends is a top priority. What's here today could be gone tomorrow. For the time we have here on earth is time borrowed. Use it wisely. Treat yourself and others with love, respect, and kindness. Dig deep within yourself and the blessing you will find it. Share it unconditionally and the fullness of the essence of life you will in return-too-receive manifestation into beautiful and pleasant memories.

Doubt

Don't let doubt kill your aspirations and dreams. Before you even try to accomplish them, into your abyss, you'll be drowning. So be confident to be all you can be. Moving forward out of the grips of stagnation and hesitation to fulfill the promises to yourself you have made and receive its fullness of your blessings.

Coveted

The road of life is paved with both failure and success. No matter how hard it may seem to travel, you must give it your absolute best. Along it you'll see many who've given up on the side of the road. Many for the shortcuts to their dreams have sold their precious soul. The thing you want most to obtain won't be easy to get. Through faith and trusting God once gotten it'll be pretty much worth it. The feeling of accomplishing your goal will be worth its weight in silver and gold. Happy you will be to have found and obtain finally your soul and that coveted inner peace.

Flourish

As winter reluctantly releases its grip on the world passing the baton to spring and its process of renewal. As the warmth cracks the coldness, optimism fills the air as flowers begin their full journey to beautify the world. For many inhabitants, it's the chance to work, preparing for promoting the selfless act for the overall survival and wellness of the species. We can learn a valuable lesson from the beauty of all the living things around us. For the positive advancement and betterment of the future of humanity, we must wholeheartedly prepare now so we can continue to flourish by example for all to see.

Freely Flow

Life is a path full of known and unknown discoveries and, in most cases, the spiritual eye is needed to unravel many of its mysteries. Time plays a pivotal role maturing man to his ultimate height of growth. Synchronizing the basic elements, wisdom, knowledge, and understanding of the soul in which all answers freely flow.

God's Call

Love and its simplistic principles are never ending and has the enchanting power of nurturing, healing, and mending back together broken hearts and broken souls— removing all doubts, negativity, and darkness so positivity, hope, and light can flow and brightly glow. Able to see the beauty in all things: giving joy and harmony to the birds' melodies in unison as they sing. Bringing about within each and all the ability to lift oneself out of the dismal and back into the race heeding to God's call.

Happier Days

When one door closes, another one opens. Don't be hesitant or afraid to walk through it, as it can provide all the things you've been diligently praying and hoping for. You may seem from past experiences drained, down, and out but wholeheartedly trust God almighty and you'll come up victorious, standing triumphantly in his glory and sharing and blessing others of your spiritual journey; How hope, strength and perseverance have helped you along the road that is somewhat treacherous along the way but no matter what, you kept your eyes on the prize leading to a brighter future and happier days.

Life's Strokes

A new day is beginning to stake its claim on the world's horizon as rain falling from the opening of the mystic and awesome sky and clouds replenishes the grateful and ready scenery, composing musical tones as they cascade along the surface. The midst brings about a renewal of the agreement between the two entities that has been agreed upon and signed into fruition and without due, fulfilled. Spreading its enlightenment and ever so sustaining happiness throughout and painting on the canvas the composition of life differently, each day much more. Mesmerizing, elegantly and beautifully seen through the spiritual eye than previously before.

Pieces

In the abyss of my empty mind was where I spent alone most of the time. Within its corridors, I walked hand in hand with darkness. I was blinded by its lure of stagnation. I became satisfied on its dietary mixture of vanity. The more I consumed, the less I became, engulfed by the insanity which was my life. I fell into the endless bottom of strife. I wanted so badly to reach out to someone, anyone. I genuinely believed that I was done. Out of the madness that I self-created within the boundaries of my own counsel and understanding. I was surprised that I was still standing. God had for me a purpose and the more I tried to run away from it, over time, from the ashes, it would surface. Now, grateful am I to be no more fighting against his will. My purpose here on earth, I am ready, able, and willing to fulfill: on the hill, being that light so others too can pick up the pieces, live out their purpose and for his glory their life.

Pit

The higher intellect for centuries has softly spoken to humanity. Words of wisdom are meant to keep it from the grips of insanity. Rainbows are the constant reminder in the sky that his intellect is manifested in our existence and lives. Our faith is based on this fact that searching for the intangible blessings, there would be nothing we would lack. Humanity uses the intellect you have freely been given to uplift yourself that you've fallen into, out of the miry pit.

Presence

In the abyss of self is where I felt at home. Where my deepest and darkest desires and thoughts freely roamed. I was in so much pain and denial that to fill this hole I relied on outside entities. The more I filled it up, the more I became lost and so empty from within. I had serious problems and felt, no matter how much I tried reaching out, there was nothing or no one that could solve them. When I was about to give up on life, you—suddenly—Lord, out of nowhere appeared. Through the darkness, I could finally see a light. My burdens you took, and my load was lightened and set my feet on a new road. Now within me, your love fuels my soul in which it grows and grows. Now those who doubted the power of the Lord can now, through me, see the presence of Him now and forever more.

Through it All

The pandemic of violence has long been a thorn in the rib of humanity. It seems that there's no solution to this insanity. Greed and self-hatred play an integral part in its manifestation. Slowly but surely, it is bound to lead to man's annihilation. This world is ours to abundantly share but the stress and mishap misuse of its vast resources, I don't know how much more of it, it can truly take or even bear. There's still a chance for us all to do our part positively, daily and instead of just talking about it, there is a point where we just must start. The road isn't going to be easy but if we are dedicated to its cause, the power of love will finally see us as one humanity successfully through it all.

Vital

Humanity, how can we continue to live with ourselves. Unfortunately, we love to cause one another misery, strife and pain and hit below the humane belt. Life is a constant struggle and battle. It's even worse that with hatred, prejudice, and inequality, this too is on my back, I have to saddle. Why can't we put away the nonessential and just learn to get along? Aren't you tired, humanity, of listening to the same ole damn song? We all have a divine purpose. It's to promote for the betterment of our wholeness, a cause very worthy and profound that's deep within the layers of our divine surface. Follow the humble ways of the industrious ant. Despite its differences, for the colony, it goes about its duty with joy and happiness, without the disrespect and insane rant. It knows that no matter how much it does, it's counted within the excess and share, equally among the colonies stronghold to promote its greatness. We, as human, in the scheme of the greatness of humanity and our survival, must learn to work together for the betterment of our species, promoting and sharing love that is most vital.

Lisa Tomey

Adjusting Lenses

humankind's nature

often means brisking each day

keeping steady pace

what happens when it changes

when the leaves of life falter

as the elder man

finds the keys don't play as well

hearing notes less clear

it's an evolvement of life

requiring tune ups often

when grandmothers cry
because their children are old
no longer in laps
still wanting for the snuggles
take them back to the time when

as life slows way down
keeping in mind the goodness
days when suns are high
looking to the skies for hope
seeing joyfulness each day

adjusting lenses
early in the children's lives
seeing and learning
each day is perfectly made
for any age to delight

Frozen Release

Tanka Train

frozen in her thoughts

how could she find sweet release

or any relief

some things have a stronger grip

than what anyone can see

grasping for answers

how to chisel away ice

frozen in her veins

solidifying ice slabs

glossing over the secrets

voices from beyond

calling to her soul to free

strengthening numbers

ready to help set her free

lending, giving their powers

the breaths of millions

feeling the fiery heartbeats

raging for lost souls

escaping the prison cell

escaping the torturous

many voices speaking

telling of the hope for peace

one listening soul

knowing there is true freedom

in breaking free of lost dreams

tempered to resolve

place the anvil on the ground

forged on a new life

allow the frozen to thaw

step forward to make new life

Grateful

Grateful for living

Happy for the days that come

Giving hope to life

Easy to be easy it seems

Harder to be spirited

The soul wants happy

The heart wants to sing along

Pumping red iron

Giving beats to keep going

But why is it so hard, now?

It's appearances

It's looking like it's easy

It's making the moves

One step in front of others

Yet, the spirit is dying

What will it take, life?

What will make it flow better?

What will drive the force?

Seems the spirit just lingers

Pushing forth for making hope

Sighs become begats

Tongues unite in spirit songs

Once again breathe in

Let the tempos flow so strong

Healing comes with slow, sweet song

The beat is tapping

Feel it working from the feet

Giving it a chance

Flowing throughout to the soul

How can this be so, so true?

Feel it in your heart

Beating in rhythms own time

Lungs have reached their fill

Life unites within the flesh

With spirits grateful, rising

Kindness Calls

haiku train
it's nature's call
flowering to openness
wanting your wonder

wonder brings hoping
opening the eyes widely
seeing nature's needs

kindness calls your name
taking steps to help the world
one heart at a time

Spend One Day

Spend one day

seeking ways to help

looking for the lost

bringing them home

home to your heart

home to your soul

showing kindness

the natural way

What do you see?

Are there people in need?

No matter where you look

there's someone to see

eyes open and heart and soul too

keeping your focus on ways to do well

kindness will come to you

when you seek to be the one to help

Spend one day

and you will find

there's much more need

and little time

so, seek the ways

to help those others

after all

we are all sisters and brothers

After one day

it will be hard

not seeing needs

and that's how it starts

looking for ways

the ways will find you

opening the mind

to possibility

servitude comes natural to you

How You Feel When You Help Someone

Once, I was told
by an incredibly wise man
when we do kindness for others
we do it for ourselves

Pondering those words
at first, I was confused
I always thought
it was just the right thing to do

Reflecting his words
I must admit
it does feel good
to help someone

Supposing he's right
and likely he is
doing kindness to others
means kindness to you

103

Passing the Impossible

As each day seemed to run into the other
it seemed impossible to rise and shine.
Covers over my head, feeling despair,
my exhausted mind gave way.

Depression set in for a long winter
as each day was just a lull,
when thoughts turned to endings
from this life of certain dismay.

Seeking answers was hard
when it did not seem possible
to pull through this darkness
when light was too far to reach.

There was a glimmer of hope
when I looked in the mirror—
looking back at me
was a willing participant.

To get back my life I had to reflect

what parts to keep and what to leave.

When I found there was just one thing

to pull me out from this disdain.

Just one thing to pull me through

to get out of the darkness,

to find the place I was needed,

I searched inside and found one thing.

That one thing led to another.

I started to see that there was hope.

It may have been a spark of a glimmer

but it was enough to help me through.

Author's Note: *This may sound simple, but I can tell you from my own personal experience with depression, that even the smallest sliver of hope means something. It means that we get to enjoy the essence of one more day with you. And this, my friend, is enough.*

Shimmer

shimmering in light

of the shadows of the eve

sparkle not under

but allowing the sprinkles

of stars from the sweet night's shine

can this be so true

to allow such a glimmer

of hope to the night

knowing that waking in the

shadows of last night's sweet dreams

is this such a hope

that brings softness to this life

and allows sweetness

to touch the tip of the tongue

and leave sweet tastes of honey

Climbing the Stairs - Hope for Generations

stairs were fun when we were young

adventurous as we crawled, then

ran up oh so fast

at four, I tumbled downstairs

it was my first memory

funny thing about

stairs, how they take us up and

down we go again

it's kind of like life, you know

there are ascents and descents

taking the first steps

is such a challenge to do

also, to observe

cajoling along the way

making sure they climb safely

once they are alone

taking their own steps, choices

going up and down

how we want to be there and hold

hands out like we're banisters

letting them go free

is one of the toughest things

but oh, so vital

to watch their independence

wishing they would hold your hands

holding them in hearts

keeping watch and being there

just enough to show

they have got this, and they know

you are going to be there

then there comes a time

when you're not so much around

when they're on their own

and you trust that all you've done

is enough and hope it's true

and before you know

they are helping someone else

crawling up those stairs

holding hands and guiding them

it's the circle of dear life

when you are the one

who needs help as you ascend

trusting they will be

holding you close in their hearts

and the world moves at your pace

you will know the life

as the descent comes for sure

where the light still shines

from the glow of your most dear

as you make that final climb

The Spirit of Music Plays On

as I look at the tan shaded keys of the piano

crackled dingey and peeling

melodies are now memories

of the time when elegance was about tea and piano time

when we all dressed proper and sang deep from the soul

just as when we faced the hurricanes

we gathered at the farm

secured the property

gathered by the waiting piano

until the master touched the keys

and all worries of wind and rain

were belted out to calm the storms

and we survived

our dear piano survived

always leaving us with peace

each day was another day of hope

ballads and nursery tunes alike

grew the spirit

another moment to survive

another moment to love

and as we faced the pandemic

the old soul piano was still there with us

some have passed on

but the music remained

it comforted us as we once again gathered

and realized that all the riches of the world

could not do more than the riches of knowing

we had each other

we still had music

we still had soul

looking at the old piano

abandoned by time and loss

I leave a yellow rose of joy

for time has leant more than anything else

and I am grateful for the song

ABOUT THE AUTHORS

LaVan Robinson is a veteran who believes in his country. He has an adult son, Audy, to whom he devotes his writing. LaVan took his mother's maiden name as his last name in her honor.

LaVan has four books of poetry published and has plans for at least one more. He has also contributed to *Fine Lines Literary Journal* and to *Heart Beats – Anthology of Poetry* and is a regular contributor to online magazines. All his books are available on Amazon.

He can be found at one of the many open mics when he is not fishing. LaVan is also on Social Media.

Lisa Tomey resides in North Carolina. She is manager of Prolific Pulse Press LLC.

She has published *Heart Beats – Anthology of Poetry* (2021) and *Heart Sounds* (2018) available on Amazon.

Her work has appeared in several publications, including *Fine Lines Literary Journal*, where she is an editor.

She can be found on Medium and Social Media.

A poetry editor, she believes in helping others bring forth the best of their work.

Her press was created as a passion to helping poets publish their fine works.

www.ingramcontent.com/pod-product-compliance
Lightning Source LLC
Chambersburg PA
CBHW071558040426
42452CB00008B/1216